ISBN 978-1-332-78627-5
PIBN 10448001

1 MONTH OF
FREE
READING

at

www.ForgottenBooks.com

By purchasing this book you are eligible for one month membership to ForgottenBooks.com, giving you unlimited access to our entire collection of over 700,000 titles via our web site and mobile apps.

To claim your free month visit:

www.forgottenbooks.com/free448001

English
Français
Deutsche
Italiano
Español
Português

www.forgottenbooks.com

Mythology Photography **Fiction**
Fishing Christianity **Art** Cooking
Essays Buddhism Freemasonry
Medicine **Biology** Music **Ancient
Egypt** Evolution Carpentry Physics
Dance Geology **Mathematics** Fitness
Shakespeare **Folklore** Yoga Marketing
Confidence Immortality Biographies
Poetry **Psychology** Witchcraft
Electronics Chemistry History **Law**
Accounting **Philosophy** Anthropology
Alchemy Drama Quantum Mechanics
Atheism Sexual Health **Ancient History**
Entrepreneurship Languages Sport
Paleontology Needlework Islam
Metaphysics Investment Archaeology
Parenting Statistics Criminology
Motivational

ECHOES OF LIFE AND DEATH
XLVII LYRICS

The summer's flower is to the summer sweet,
Though to itself it only live and die.

SHAKESPEARE.

ECHOES OF LIFE AND DEATH FORTY-SEVEN LYRICS BY WILLIAM ERNEST HENLEY

PORTLAND MAINE
THOMAS B MOSHER
MDCCCCVIII

TO MY WIFE

Take, dear, my little sheaf of songs,
    For, old or new,
All that is good in them belongs
    Only to you;

And, singing as when all was young,
    They will recall
Those others, lived but left unsung —
    The best of all.

W. E. H.

April, 1888
  September, 1897.

ECHOES OF LIFE AND DEATH

1872-1889

Aquí está encerrada el alma del licenciado Pedro Garcías.

GIL BLAS AU LECTEUR.

I

TO MY MOTHER

HIMING a dream by the way
   With ocean's rapture and roar,
I met a maiden to-day
   Walking alone on the shore:
Walking in maiden wise,
  Modest and kind and fair,
The freshness of spring in her eyes
  And the fulness of spring in her hair.

Cloud-shadow and scudding sun-burst
  Were swift on the floor of the sea,
And a mad wind was romping its worst,
  But what was their magic to me?
Or the charm of the midsummer skies?
  I only saw she was there,
A dream of the sea in her eyes
  And the kiss of the sea in her hair.

I watched her vanish in space;
   She came where I walked no more;
But something had passed of her grace
   To the spell of the wave and the shore;
And now, as the glad stars rise,
   She comes to me, rosy and rare,
The delight of the wind in her eyes
   And the hand of the wind in her hair.

L IFE is bitter.   All the faces of the years,
    Young and old, are gray with travail and
      with tears.
  Must we only wake to toil, to tire, to weep?
In the sun, among the leaves, upon the flowers,
Slumber stills to dreamy death the heavy
      hours . . .
            Let me sleep.

Riches won but mock the old, unable years;
Fame's a pearl that hides beneath a sea of tears;
  Love must wither, or must live alone and weep.
In the sunshine, through the leaves, across the flowers,
While we slumber, death approaches through
      the hours . . .
            Let me sleep.

III

O, GATHER me the rose, the rose,
   While yet in flower we find it,
For summer smiles, but summer goes,
   And winter waits behind it!

For with the dream foregone, foregone,
   The deed forborne for ever,
The worm, regret, will canker on,
   And Time will turn him never.

So well it were to love, my love,
   And cheat of any laughter
The fate beneath us and above,
   The dark before and after.

The myrtle and the rose, the rose,
   The sunshine and the swallow,
The dream that comes, the wish that goes,
   The memories that follow!

IV

I. M.

R. T. HAMILTON BRUCE

(1846–1899)

OUT of the night that covers me,
　　Black as the Pit from pole to pole,
I thank whatever gods may be
　　For my unconquerable soul.

In the fell clutch of circumstance
　　I have not winced nor cried aloud.
Under the bludgeonings of chance
　　My head is bloody, but unbowed.

Beyond this place of wrath and tears
　　Looms but the Horror of the shade,
And yet the menace of the years
　　Finds, and shall find, me unafraid.

It matters not how strait the gate,
　　How charged with punishments the scroll,
I am the master of my fate ·
　　I am the captain of my soul.

I AM the Reaper.
    All things with heedful hook
Silent I gather.
Pale roses touched with the spring,
Tall corn in summer,
Fruits rich with autumn, and frail winter blos
Reaping, still reaping —
All things with heedful hook
Timely I gather.

I am the Sower.
All the unbodied life
Runs through my seed-sheet.
Atom with atom wed,
Each quickening the other,
Fall through my hands, ever changing, still cha
Ceaselessly sowing,
Life, incorruptible life,
Flows from my seed-sheet.

Maker and breaker,
I am the ebb and the flood,
Here and Hereafter.
Sped through the tangle and coil
Of infinite nature,

Viewless and soundless I fashion all being.
Taker and giver,
I am the womb and the grave,
The Now and the Ever.

PRAISE the generous gods for giving
  In a world of wrath and strife,
With a little time for living,
  Unto all the joy of life.

At whatever source we drink it,
  Art or love or faith or wine,
In whatever terms we think it,
  It is common and divine.

Praise the high gods, for in giving
  This to man, and this alone,
They have made his chance of living
  Shine the equal of their own.

VII

FILL a glass with golden wine,
　　And the while your lips are wet
Set their perfume unto mine,
　　And forget,
Every kiss we take and give
Leaves us less of life to live.

Yet again! Your whim and mine
　In a happy while have met.
All your sweets to me resign,
　　Nor regret
That we press with every breath,
Sighed or singing, nearer death.

WE'LL go no more a-roving by the light
of the moon.
November glooms are barren beside the dusk of
June.
The summer flowers are faded, the summer
thoughts are sere.
We'll go no more a-roving, lest worse befall,
my dear.

We'll go no more a-roving by the light of the
moon.
The song we sang rings hollow, and heavy
runs the tune.
Glad ways and words remembered would
shame the wretched year.
We'll go no more a-roving, nor dream we did,
my dear.

We'll go no more a-roving by the light of the
moon.
If yet we walk together, we need not shun the
moon.
No sweet thing left to savour, no sad thing left
to fear,
We'll go no more a-roving, but weep at home,
my dear.

IX

To W. R.

MADAM Life's a piece in bloom
    Death goes dogging everywhere
She's the tenant of the room,
    He's the ruffian on the stair.

You shall see her as a friend,
    You shall bilk him once and twice;
But he'll trap you in the end,
    And he'll stick you for her price.

With his kneebones at your chest,
    And his knuckles in your throat,
You would reason — plead — protest!
    Clutching at her petticoat;

But she's heard it all before,
    Well she knows you've had your fun,
Gingerly she gains the door,
    And your little job is done.

THE sea is full of wandering foam,
    The sky of driving cloud ;
My restless thoughts among them roam
    The night is dark and loud.

Where are the hours that came to me
    So beautiful and bright?
A wild wind shakes the wilder sea
    O, dark and loud's the night!

XI

To W. R.

THICK is the darkness —
    Sunward, O, sunward !
Rough is the highway —
    Onward, still onward !

Dawn harbours surely
    East of the shadows.
Facing us somewhere
    Spread the sweet meadows.

Upward and forward !
    Time will restore us
Light is above us,
    Rest is before us.

XII

TO me at my fifth-floor window
   The chimney-pots in rows
Are sets of pipes pandean
   For every wind that blows;

And the smoke that whirls and eddies
   In a thousand times and keys
Is really a visible music
   Set to my reveries.

O monstrous pipes, melodious
   With fitful tune and dream,
The clouds are your only audience,
   Her thought is your only theme!

BRING her again, O western wind,
　　Over the western sea :
Gentle and good and fair and kind,
　　Bring her again to me !

Not that her fancy holds me dear,
　　Not that a hope may be :
Only that I may know her near,
　　Wind of the western sea.

THE wan sun westers, faint and slow;
    The eastern distance glimmers gray;
An eerie haze comes creeping low
Across the little, lonely bay;
And from the sky-line far away
About the quiet heaven are spread
Mysterious hints of dying day,
Thin, delicate dreams of green and red.

And weak, reluctant surges lap
And rustle round and down the strand.
No other sound . . . If it should hap,
The ship that sails from fairy-land!
The silken shrouds with spells are manned,
The hull is magically scrolled,
The squat mast lives, and in the sand
The gold prow-griffin claws a hold.

It steals to seaward silently;
Strange fish-folk follow thro' the gloom;
Great wings flap overhead; I see
The Castle of the Drowsy Doom
Vague thro' the changeless twilight loom,
Enchanted, hushed.   And ever there
She slumbers in eternal bloom,
Her cushions hid with golden hair.

XV

THERE is a wheel inside my head
　　Of wantonness and wine,
　An old, cracked fiddle is begging without,
But the wind with scents of the sea is fed,
　And the sun seems glad to shine.

The sun and the wind are akin to you,
　As you are akin to June.
　　But the fiddle! . . . It giggles and twit-
　　　ters about,
And, love and laughter! who gave him the
　　cue? —
　He's playing your favourite tune.

WHILE the west is paling
    Starshine is begun.
While the dusk is failing
    Glimmers up the sun.

So, till darkness cover
    Life's retreating gleam,
Lover follows lover,
    Dream succeeds to dream.

Stoop to my endeavour,
    O my love, and be
Only and for ever
    Sun and stars to me.

XVII

THE sands are alive with sunshine,
  The bathers lounge and throng,
And out in the bay a bugle
  Is lilting a gallant song.

The clouds go racing eastward,
  The blithe wind cannot rest,
And a shard on the shingle flashes
  Like the shining soul of a jest;

While children romp in the surges,
  And sweethearts wander free,
And the Firth as with laughter dimples
  I would it were deep over me !

To A. D.

THE nightingale has a lyre of gold,
    The lark's is a clarion call,
And the blackbird plays but a boxwood flute,
    But I love him best of all.

For his song is all of the joy of life,
    And we in the mad, spring weather,
We two have listened till he sang
    Our hearts and lips together.

XIX

YOUR heart has trembled to my tongue,
　　Your hands in mine have lain,
Your thought to me has leaned and clung,
　　　　Again and yet again,
　　　　My dear,
　　　　Again and yet again.

Now die the dream, or come the wife,
　　˙The past is not in vain,
For wholly as it was your life
　　　　Can never be again,
　　　　My dear,
　　　　Can never be again.

XX

THE surges gushed and sounded,
    The blue was the blue of June,
And low above the brightening east
    Floated a shred of moon.

The woods were black and solemn,
    The night winds large and free,
And in your thought a blessing seemed
    To fall on land and sea.

WE flash across the level.
　　We thunder thro' the bridges.
We bicker down the cuttings.
　　We sway along the ridges.

A rush of streaming hedges,
　　Of jostling lights and shadows,
Of hurtling, hurrying stations,
　　Of racing woods and meadows.

We charge the tunnels headlong —
　　The blackness roars and shatters.
We crash between embankments —
　　The open spins and scatters.

We shake off the miles like water,
　　We might carry a royal ransom;
And I think of her waiting, waiting,
　　And long for a common hansom.

XXII

THE West a glimmering lake of light,
　　A dream of pearly weather,
The first of stars is burning white —
　　The star we watch together.
Is April dead?　The unresting year
　　Will shape us our September,
And April's work is done, my dear —
　　Do you not remember?

O gracious eve! O happy star,
　　Still-flashing, glowing, sinking! —
Who lives of lovers near or far
　　So glad as I in thinking?
The gallant world is warm and green,
　　For May fulfils November.
When lights and leaves and loves have been,
　　Sweet, will you remember?

O star benignant and serene,
　　I take the good to-morrow,
That fills from verge to verge my dream,
　　With all its joy and sorrow!
The old, sweet spell is unforgot
　　That turns to June December;
And, tho' the world remembered not,
　　Love, we would remember.

THE skies are strown with stars,
　　The streets are fresh with dew,
A thin moon drifts to westward,
The night is hushed and cheerful:
　My thought is quick with you.

Near windows gleam and laugh,
　And far away a train
Clanks glowing through the stillness:
A great content's in all things,
　And life is not in vain.

THE full sea rolls and thunders
    In glory and in glee.
O, bury me not in the senseless earth
    But in the living sea!

Ay, bury me where it surges
    A thousand miles from shore,
And in its brotherly unrest
    I'll range for evermore.

IN the year that's come and gone, love, his
    flying feather
Stooping slowly, gave us heart, and bade us
    walk together.
In the year that's coming on, though many a
    troth be broken,
We at least will not forget aught that love
    hath spoken.

In the year that's come and gone, dear, we
    wove a tether
All of gracious words and thoughts, binding
    two together.
In the year that's coming on with its wealth of
    roses
We shall weave it stronger yet, ere the circle
    closes.

In the year that's come and gone, in the golden
    weather,
Sweet, my sweet, we swore to keep the watch
    of life together.
In the year that's coming on, rich in joy and
    sorrow,
We shall light our lamp, and wait life's mys-
    terious morrow.

XXVI

IN the placid summer midnight,
    Under the drowsy sky,
I seem to hear in the stillness
    The moths go glimmering by.

One by one from the windows
    The lights have all been sped.
Never a blind looks conscious —
    The street is asleep in bed !

But I come where a living casement
    Laughs luminous and wide ;
I hear the song of a piano
    Break in a sparkling tide ;

And I feel, in the waltz that frolics
    And warbles swift and clear,
A sudden sense of shelter
    And friendliness and cheer

A sense of tinkling glasses,
    Of love and laughter and light —
The piano stops, and the window
    Stares blank out into the night.

The blind goes out, and I wander
  To the old, unfriendly sea,
The lonelier for the memory
  That walks like a ghost with me.

SHE sauntered by the swinging seas,
   A jewel glittered at her ear,
And, teasing her along, the breeze
   Brought many a rounded grace more near.

So passing, one with wave and beam,
   She left for memory to caress
A laughing thought, a golden gleam,
   A hint of hidden loveliness.

XXVIII

To S. C.

BLITHE dreams arise to greet us,
　　And life feels clean and new,
For the old love comes to meet us
　　In the dawning and the dew.
O'erblown with sunny shadows,
　　O'ersped with winds at play,
The woodlands and the meadows
　　Are keeping holiday.
Wild foals are scampering, neighing,
　　Brave merles their hautboys blow ·
Come ! let us go a-maying
　　As in the Long-Ago.

Here we but peak and dwindle :
　　The clank of chain and crane,
The whir of crank and spindle
　　Bewilder heart and brain ;
The ends of our endeavour
　　Are merely wealth and fame,
Yet in the still Forever
　　We're one and all the same ;
Delaying, still delaying,
　　We watch the fading west :

Come! let us go a-maying,
　　Nor fear to take the best.

Yet beautiful and spacious
　　The wise, old world appears.
Yet frank and fair and gracious
　　Outlaugh the jocund years.
Our arguments disputing,
　　The universal Pan.
Still wanders fluting — fluting —
　　Fluting to maid and man.
Our weary well-a-waying
　　His music cannot still:
Come! let us go a-maying,
　　And pipe with him our fill.

Where wanton winds are flowing
　　Among the gladdening grass;
Where hawthorn brakes are blowing,
　　And meadow perfumes pass;
Where morning's grace is greenest,
　　And fullest noon's of pride;
Where sunset spreads serenest,
　　And sacred night's most wide;
Where nests are swaying, swaying,
　　And spring's fresh voices call,
Come! let us go a-maying,
　　And bless the God of all!

XXIX

To R. L. S.

A CHILD,
   Curious and innocent,
Slips from his Nurse, and rejoicing
Loses himself in the Fair.

Thro' the jostle and din
Wandering, he revels,
Dreaming, desiring, possessing;
Till, of a sudden
Tired and afraid, he beholds
The sordid assemblage
Just as it is; and he runs
With a sob to his Nurse
(Lighting at last on him),
And in her motherly bosom
Cries him to sleep.

Thus thro' the World,
Seeing and feeling and knowing,
Goes Man: till at last,
Tired of experience, he turns
To the friendly and comforting breast
Of the old nurse, Death.

XXX

KATE-A-WHIMSIES, John-a-Dreams,
   Still debating, still delay,
And the world's a ghost that gleams —
   Wavers — vanishes away!

We must live while live we can;
   We should love while love we may.
Dread in women, doubt in man
   So the Infinite runs away.

O, HAVE you blessed, behind the stars,
  The blue sheen in the skies,
When June the roses round her calls? —
Then do you know the light that falls
  From her belovèd eyes.

And have you felt the sense of peace
  That morning meadows give? —
Then do you know the spirit of grace,
The angel abiding in her face,
  Who makes it good to live.

She shines before me, hope and dream,
  So fair, so still, so wise,
That, winning her, I seem to win
Out of the dust and drive and din
  A nook of Paradise.

XXXII

To D. H.

O, FALMOUTH is a fine town with
ships in the bay,
And I wish from my heart it's there I was
to-day;
I wish from my heart I was far away from
here,
Sitting in my parlour and talking to my dear.
For it's home, dearie, home — it's home
I want to be.
Our topsails are hoisted, and we'll away
to sea.
O, the oak and the ash and the bonnie
birken tree
They're all growing green in the old
countrie.

In Baltimore a-walking a lady I did meet
With her babe on her arm, as she came down
the street;
And I thought how I sailed, and the cradle
standing ready
For the pretty little babe that has never seen its
daddie.
And it's home, dearie, home

O, if it be a lass, she shall wear a golden ring ;
And if it be a lad, he shall fight for his king ·
With his dirk and his hat and his little jacket
     blue
He shall walk the quarter-deck as his daddie
     used to do.
     And it's home, dearie, home

O, there's a wind a-blowing, a-blowing from
     the west,
And that of all the winds is the one I like the
     best,
For it blows at our backs, and it shakes our
     pennon free,
And it soon will blow us home to the old
     countrie.
     For it's home, dearie, home — it's home
     I want to be.
     Our topsails are hoisted, and we'll away
     to sea.
     O, the oak and the ash and the bonnie
     birken tree
     They're all growing green in the old
     countrie.

NOTE. — The burthen and the third stanza are old.

XXXIII

THE ways are green with the gladdening
    sheen
  Of the young year's fairest daughter.
O, the shadows that fleet o'er the springing
    wheat!
  O, the magic of running water!
The spirit of spring is in every thing,
  The banners of spring are streaming,
We march to a tune from the fifes of June,
  And life's a dream worth dreaming.

It's all very well to sit and spell
  At the lesson there's no gainsaying;
But what the deuce are wont and use
  When the whole mad world's a-maying?
When the meadow glows, and the orchard
    snows,
  And the air's with love-motes teeming,
When fancies break, and the senses wake,
  O, life's a dream worth dreaming!

What Nature has writ with her lusty wit
  Is worded so wisely and kindly
That whoever has dipped in her manuscript
  Must up and follow her blindly.

Now the summer prime is her blithest rhyme
    In the being and the seeming,
And they that have heard the overword
    Know life's a dream worth dreaming.

XXXIV

To K. DE M.

Love blows as the wind blows,
Love blows into the heart.

NILE BOAT-SONG.

LIFE in her creaking shoes
    Goes, and more formal grows,
A round of calls and cues :
Love blows as the wind blows.
Blows ! . . . in the quiet close
As in the roaring mart,
By ways no mortal knows
Love blows into the heart.

The stars some cadence use,
Forthright the river flows,
In order fall the dews,
Love blows as the wind blows :
Blows !   and what reckoning shows
The courses of his chart?
A spirit that comes and goes,
Love blows into the heart.

XXXV

I. M.

MARGARITÆ SORORIS

(1886)

A LATE lark twitters from the quiet skies ;
        And from the west,
Where the sun, his day's work ended,
Lingers as in content,
There falls on the old, gray city
An influence luminous and serene,
A shining peace.

The smoke ascends
In a rosy-and-golden haze.   The spires
Shine, and are changed.   In the valley
Shadows rise.   The lark sings on.   The sun,
Closing his benediction,
Sinks, and the darkening air
Thrills with a sense of the triumphing night —
Night with her train of stars
And her great gift of sleep.

So be my passing !
My task accomplished and the long day done,

My wages taken, and in my heart
Some late lark singing,
Let me be gathered to the quiet west,
The sundown splendid and serene,
Death.

I GAVE my heart to a woman —
  I gave it her, branch and root.
She bruised, she wrung, she tortured
  She cast it under foot.

Under her feet she cast it,
  She trampled it where it fell,
She broke it all to pieces,
  And each was a clot of hell.

There in the rain and the sunshine
  They lay and smouldered long;
And each, when again she viewed them,
  Had turned to a living song.

XXXVII

To W. A.

OR ever the knightly years were gone
   With the old world to the grave,
I was a King in Babylon
   And you were a Christian Slave.

I saw, I took, I cast you by,
   I bent and broke your pride.
You loved me well, or I heard them lie,
   But your longing was denied.
Surely I knew that by and by
   You cursed your gods and died.

And a myriad suns have set and shone
   Since then upon the grave
Decreed by the King in Babylon
   To her that had been his Slave.

The pride I trampled is now my scathe,
   For it tramples me again.
The old resentment lasts like death,
   For you love, yet you refrain.
I break my heart on your hard unfaith,
   And I break my heart in vain.

Yet not for an hour do I wish undone
    The deed beyond the grave,
When I was a King in Babylon
    And you were a Virgin Slave.

XXXVIII

ON the way to Kew,
    By the river old and gray,
Where in the Long Ago
We laughed and loitered so,
I met a ghost to-day,
A ghost that told of you —
A ghost of low replies
And sweet, inscrutable eyes
Coming up from Richmond
As you used to do.

By the river old and gray,
The enchanted Long Ago
Murmured and smiled anew.
On the way to Kew,
March had the laugh of May,
The bare boughs looked aglow,
And old, immortal words
Sang in my breast like birds,
Coming up from Richmond
As I used with you.

With the life of Long Ago
Lived my thought of you.
By the river old and gray
Flowing his appointed way

As I watched I knew
What is so good to know —
Not in vain, not in vain,
Shall I look for you again
Coming up from Richmond
On the way to Kew.

THE Past was goodly once, and yet, when
    all is said,
The best of it we know is that it's done and
    dead.

Dwindled and faded quite, perished beyond
    recall,
Nothing is left at last of what one time was all.

Coming back like a ghost, staring and lingering
    on,
Never a word it speaks but proves it dead and
    gone.

Duty and work and joy — these things it cannot
    give ;
And the Present is life, and life is good to live.

Let it lie where it fell, far from the living sun,
The Past that, goodly once, is gone and dead and
    done.

XL

THE spring, my dear,
    Is no longer spring.
Does the blackbird sing
What he sang last year?
Are the skies the old
Immemorial blue?
Or am I, or are you,
Grown cold?

Though life be change,
It is hard to bear
When the old sweet air
Sounds forced and strange.
To be out of tune,
Plain You and I . . .
It were better to die,
And soon!

XLI

To R. A. M. S.

THE Spirit of Wine
Sang in my glass, and I listened
With love to his odorous music,
His flushed and magnificent song.

——" I am health, I am heart, I am life !
For I give for the asking
The fire of my father, the Sun,
And the strength of my mother, the Earth.
Inspiration in essence,
I am wisdom and wit to the wise,
His visible muse to the poet,
The soul of desire to the lover,
The genius of laughter to all.

" Come, lean on me, ye that are weary !
Rise, ye faint-hearted and doubting !
Haste, ye that lag by the way !
I am Pride, the consoler ;
Valour and Hope are my henchmen ;
I am the Angel of Rest.

" I am life, I am wealth, I am fame ·
For I captain an army

Of shining and generous dreams;
And mine, too, all mine, are the keys
Of that secret spiritual shrine,
Where, his work-a-day soul put by,
Shut in with his saint of saints —
With his radiant and conquering self —
Man worships, and talks, and is glad.

"Come, sit with me, ye that are lonely,
Ye that are paid with disdain,
Ye that are chained and would soar !
I am beauty and love ;
I am friendship, the comforter ;
I am that which forgives and forgets."——

The Spirit of Wine
Sang in my heart, and I triumphed
In the savour and scent of his music,
His magnetic and mastering song.

A WINK from Hesper, falling
  Fast in the wintry sky,
Comes through the even blue,
Dear, like a word from you .
  Is it good-bye?

Across the miles between us
  I send you sigh for sigh.
Good-night, sweet friend, good-night:
Till life and all take flight,
  Never good-bye.

XLIII

FRIENDS . . old friends
  One sees how it ends.
A woman looks
Or a man tells lies,
And the pleasant brooks
And the quiet skies,
Ruined with brawling
And caterwauling,
Enchant no more
As they did before.
And so it ends
With friends.

Friends . . old friends
And what if it ends?
Shall we dare to shirk
What we live to learn?
It has done its work,
It has served its turn;
And, forgive and forget
Or hanker and fret,
We can be no more
As we were before.
When it ends, it ends
With friends.

Friends .   old friends . . .
So it breaks, so it ends.
There let it rest !
It has fought and won,
And is still the best
That either has done.
Each as he stands
The work of its hands,
Which shall be more
As he was before ? . . .
What is it ends
With friends ?

IF it should come to be,
  This proof of you and me,
    This type and sign
Of hours that smiled and shone
And yet seemed dead and gone
    As old-world wine :

Of Them Within the Gate
Ask we no richer fate,
    No boon above,
For girl child or for boy,
My gift of life and joy,
    Your gift of love.

To W. B. B.

FROM the brake the Nightingale
    Sings exulting to the Rose;
Though he sees her waxing pale
    In her passionate repose,
While she triumphs waxing frail,
    Fading even while she glows;
        Though he knows
        How it goes —
Knows of last year's Nightingale
    Dead with last year's Rose.

Wise the enamoured Nightingale,
    Wise the well-belovèd Rose!
Love and life shall still prevail,
    Nor the silence at the close
Break the magic of the tale
    In the telling, though it shows —
        Who but knows
        How it goes! —
Life a last year's Nightingale,
    Love a last year's Rose.

XLVI

MATRI DILECTISSIMÆ

I. M.

IN the waste hour
  Between to-day and yesterday
We watched, while on my arm —
Living flesh of her flesh, bone of her bone —
Dabbled in sweat the sacred head
Lay uncomplaining, still, contemptuous, strange :
Till the dear face turned dead,
And to a sound of lamentation
The good, heroic soul with all its wealth —
Its sixty years of love and sacrifice,
Suffering and passionate faith — was reabsorbed
In the inexorable Peace,
And life was changed to us for evermore.

Was nothing left of her but tears
Like blood-drops from the heart?
Nought save remorse
For duty unfulfilled, justice undone,
And charity ignored?   Nothing but love,
Forgiveness, reconcilement, where in truth,
But for this passing

Into the unimaginable abyss
These things had never been?

Nay, there were we,
Her five strong sons!
To her Death came — the great Deliverer came!
As equal comes to equal, throne to throne.
She was a mother of men.

The stars shine as of old.   The unchanging River
Bent on his errand of immortal law,
Works his appointed way
To the immemorial sea.
And the brave truth comes overwhelmingly home
That she in us yet works and shines,
Lives and fulfils herself,
Unending as the river and the stars.

Dearest, live on
In such an immortality
As we thy sons,
Born of thy body and nursed
At those wild, faithful breasts,
Can give — of generous thoughts,
And honourable words, and deeds
That make men half in love with fate!
Live on, O brave and true,
In us thy children, in ours whose life is thine —

Our best and theirs ! What is that best but the
Thee, and thy gift to us, to pass
Like light along the infinite of space
To the immitigable end?

Between the river and the stars,
O royal and radiant soul,
Thou dost return, thine influences return
Upon thy children as in life, and death
Turns stingless ! What is Death
But Life in act? How should the Unteeming G
Be victor over thee,
Mother, a mother of men?

CROSSES and troubles a-many have proved me.
    One or two women (God bless them!) have
        loved me.
I have worked and dreamed, and I've talked at will.
Of art and drink I have had my fill.
I've comforted here, and I've succoured there.
I've faced my foes, and I've backed my friends.
I've blundered, and sometimes made amends.
I have prayed for light, and I've known despair.
Now I look before, as I look behind, .
Come storm, come shine, whatever befall,
With a grateful heart and a constant mind,
For the end I know is the best of all.

INDEX TO FIRST LINES

INDEX TO FIRST LINES

NINE HUNDRED AND FIFTY COPIES OF
THIS BOOK PRINTED ON VAN GELDER
HAND-MADE PAPER AND THE TYPE
DISTRIBUTED.